HOUSES & APARTMENTS
UNDER **1000** SQUARE FEET

Edited by **Yuri Caravaca Gallardo**

HOUSES & APARTMENTS
UNDER **1000** SQUARE FEET

Edited by **Yuri Caravaca Gallardo**

FIREFLY BOOKS

A FIREFLY BOOK

Published by Firefly Books Ltd. 2013

First printing

Publisher Cataloging-in-Publication Data (U.S.)

A CIP record for this title is available from the Library of Congress

Library and Archives Canada Cataloguing in Publication

A CIP record for this title is available from Library and Archives Canada

Published in the United States by
Firefly Books (U.S.) Inc.
P.O. Box 1338, Ellicott Station
Buffalo, New York 14205

Published in Canada by
Firefly Books Ltd.
50 Staples Avenue, Unit 1
Richmond Hill, Ontario L4B 0A7

Cover design: Erin R. Holmes/Soplari Design

Printed in China

LOFT Publications, S.L.
Via Laietana, 32, 4°, of. 92
08003 Barcelona, Spain

For Loft:
Editor: Claudia Martínez Alonso
Editorial assistant: Ana Marques
Art direction:Mireia Casanovas Soley
Layout:Laia Pampalona Expósito, Cristina Simó Perales
Translation: textcase

Introduction

The world is becoming a cluster of cities, where the bulk of the world's population and wealth are concentrated. This incessant agglomeration of individuals is creating a virtually inexhaustible demand for housing that is pushing up prices. This, together with associated phenomena such as individualism and changes in family structure, makes the microdwelling the fastest growing type of residence.

If well planned, dense cities are more sustainable and efficient than sprawling cities, and the same can be said for housing. Indispensable to the city of the future, microdwellings synthesize the best of contemporary architecture: functionality, efficiency and the "less is more" philosophy of Mies van der Rohe.

Like city planning, defining the space of a compact home demands the prioritization of its inhabitants' current and potential needs, reconciling these with physical, legal and budgetary limitations. The aim is to create spaces that improve quality of life and also represent the personalities of their inhabitants. To achieve this, minimalist solutions are used for open-plan areas in order to unify spaces with complementary functions; straight lines and pure forms predominate; structures are transparent or translucent so they can let in natural light; materials are used literally; and there is a preference for monochromatic schemes and light colors.

This book is a collection of projects, ranging in size from 258 sq. ft. to 958 sq. ft. (24 m² to 89 m²). It does not claim to be an exhaustive list, but aims to showcase the most significant examples of contemporary compact residential architecture.

Chatou

258 sq. ft. / 24 m²

h2o architectes
Chatou, France
© Stéphane Chalmeau

The owners of this property proposed using the space in their previously unused backyard to build an almost independent home for their teenage son. A birch frame designed as "living furniture" acts as storage and permeates the space, bringing new life to previously inaccessible corners.

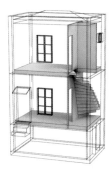

Staircase design development diagram

Dividing this narrow space into four levels multiplies useful floor space and separates it into functional areas.

This staircase turns around on itself, creating multiple landings, and is an efficient solution for maximizing the storage area without compromising circulation.

Apartments in Katayama

247/387 sq. ft. // 23/36 m²

Matsunami Mitsutomo
Katayama, Japan
© Matsunami Mitsutomo

A geometric milestone, distinctive within a prosaic cityscape, this building is a bold exercise in rationalism. The diminutive 1,200-sq.-ft. (110 m²) lot holds a building with 10 apartments: eight units and two maisonettes spread over seven floors. Its facade is almost a section of the building, emphasized by the contrast between the white and black color scheme.

The design of this facade is the result of compliance with emergency evacuation regulations, which require the presence of standard balconies.

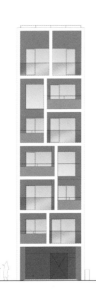

Front elevation

Building section

Floor plan options

There are three different floor plan options for the 10 apartments, each with finishes achieved by mixing materials and contrasting textures and colors.

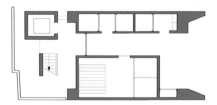

3x9 House

290 sq. ft. / 27 m²

a21studio
Ho Chi Minh City, Vietnam
© Hiroyuki Oki

Making this tiny lot habitable involved relinquishing superfluous structures in order to create a fluid space. Alternating between nature (wood)
and industry (red brick and steel) conforms with a simple and practical
language that lends cohesion to the overall space. The tree — a wholly
natural element — compensates for the hardness of the other materials.

The absence of partitions gives breadth and depth to
this space. The distribution of furniture and materials
helps to segment and define functional areas.

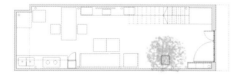

Ground floor plan

Second floor plan

The wood and red brick are well lit by the ample natural light coming in through the skylight, creating a warm, illuminated space with little stark contrast.

Expanded drawing

Mind Line

333 sq. ft. / 31 m²

Atsushi Kawamoto & Hiroki Sugiyama / mA-style architects
Yosida City, Japan
© Mayumi Kawamoto

This apartment draws a sharp contrast between the functional and more leisurely areas of the home. In the northern half, the Japanese bathroom — the only enclosed room — unites with the kitchen. This, in turn, is connected to the main room, an open multipurpose space in the southern half of the home, which culminates in large windows that open onto a porch.

The wood that runs along the floor in the main room unites the two halves of the space and is a hallmark of this home.

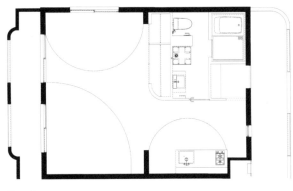

Floor plan

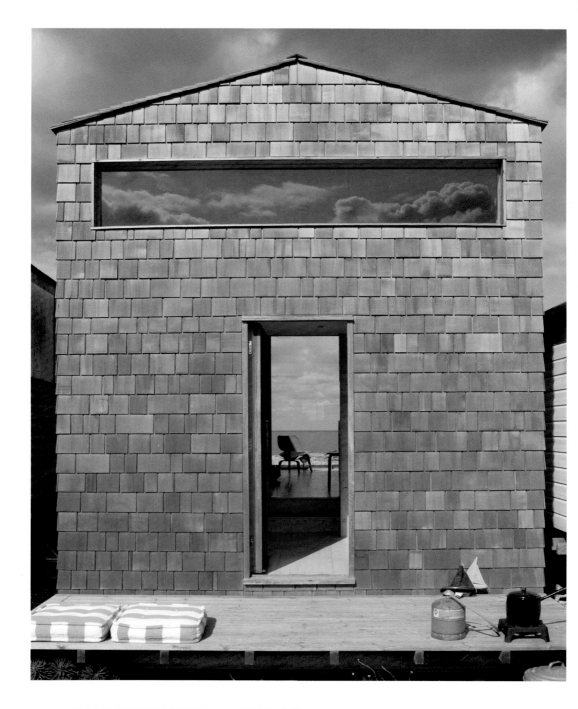

Beach Chalet

355 sq. ft. / 33 m²

Studiomama
Whitstable, UK
© Ben Anders

Like its 25 neighbors, this house is raised on galvanized steel stilts to protect it from the tides. Its cedar cladding and interior softwood lumber give it a Scandinavian feel. Not surprisingly, this coastal family retreat — one hour from London — is the work and property of Danish designer Nina Tolstrup.

High, sloped ceilings allow room for a front attic that
serves as a bedroom.

In the raised section, a huge unobstructed oblong window frames a splendid view of the sea — the vanishing point of the building.

Love House

409 sq. ft. / 38 m²

Takeshi Hosaka Architects
Yokohama, Japan
© Masao Nishikawa, Koji Fujii / Nacása & Partners Inc

The architect of this tiny house shares it with his wife. Its walls surround a space that is neither inside nor outside, in which its creator wished all of nature's elements to congregate. On the roof a delicate cleft provides its residents with a view of a portion of the sky above.

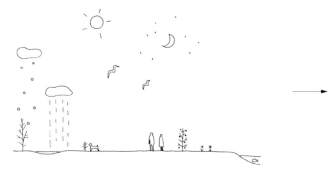

Conceptual development sketch

The curved gap in the roof displays the play of light
and shadow between sunrise and sunset.

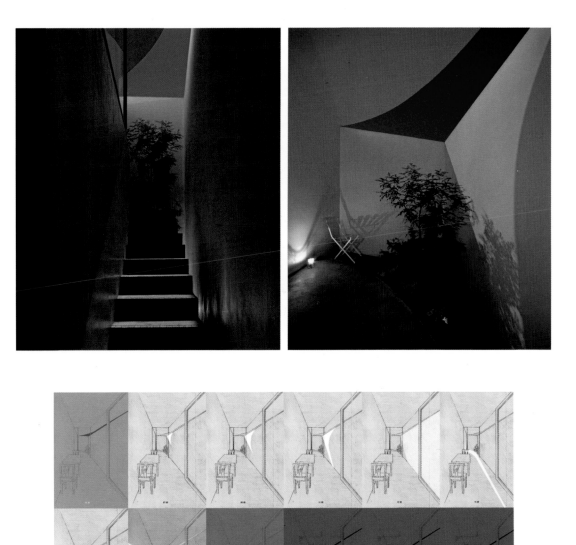

Sketches of illumination patterns

Nguyễn Huy Lượng

430 sq. ft. / 40 m²

a21studio
Ho Chi Minh City, Vietnam
© Hiroyuki Oki

The client chose this irregularly shaped lot 10 minutes from the center of town for the construction of his home and workplace. The intention was to build a green oasis in which the elements (water, light and wind) and natural plant life mix with human activity — a striking counterpoint to the polluted and hectic urban environment outside its walls.

Location plan

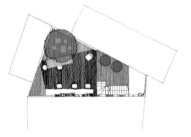

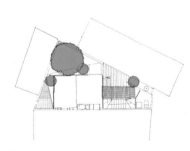

House perspective

Site plans

The wooden planks that make up the floors and stairs form a sort of membrane that filters light from the skylight on the top floor.

430-sq.-ft. Refurbishment

430 sq. ft. / 40 m²

Nir Rothem & Bosmat Sfadia Wolf / SFARO Architects
Tel Aviv, Israel
© Boaz Lavi & Jonathan Blum

Rising house prices have encouraged many homeowners to opt for remodeling. In this case, by combining all functional elements in a single, large cube at the center of the home, and dividing the remaining space into four zones, a 360° flow has been created, which improves the dwelling's livability and sense of openness.

A cube within a cube: the Matrioska structure
becomes an extremely efficient space solution.

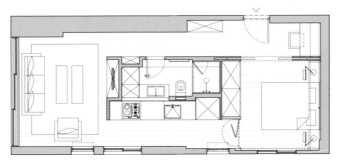

Floor plan

The sliding doors, which form part of the central cube, can be used to adjust the space according to the needs of the residents.

Casa Roc

484 sq. ft. / 45 m²

Nook Architects
Barcelona, Spain
© nieve | Productora Audiovisual

This property in the historic Gothic Quarter was found in a dilapidated state, thanks in part to successive remodeling projects. The challenge was to breathe new life into a home that had been divided into two halves by a load-bearing wall. The space was opened up but still retains some elements of its former division zones.

The kitchen is on the other side of the living room wall. The tiled floor, as well as the beams and window frames, have been restored.

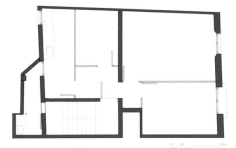

Floor plan

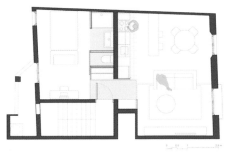

Furnished floor plan

The inner side of the wall has a contemporary feel. It complements the bathroom, which faces a bedroom with an extended gallery.

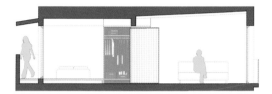

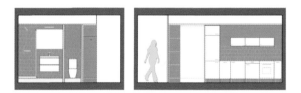

Cross and longitudinal sections

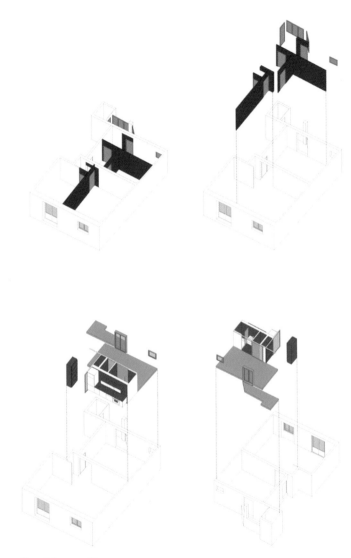

Expanded axonometrics

Appartement chez Valentin

538 sq. ft. / 50 m²

ecdm – emmanuel combarel dominique marrec
Mountrouge, France
© Gaston Bergeret

The veteran artist and owner of this property wanted to give it a face lift, the only requirement being an independent bedroom, which floats between the two levels in this space. Visible from the entrance, this bedroom seems more like an inviting island retreat than the private, secluded space typical of many bedrooms.

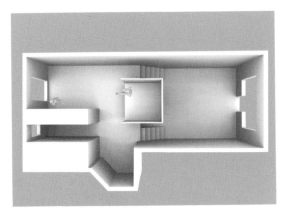

3-D floor plan

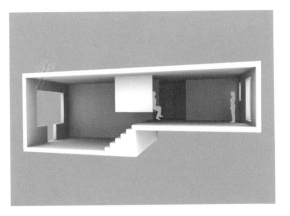

3-D longitudinal section

The "box" that houses the bedroom acts as a visual screen, and paradoxically makes the living room the most private area of the house.

House in Horinouchi

592 sq. ft. / 55 m²

Kota Mizuishi / Mizuishi Architect Atelier
Tokyo, Japan
© Hiroshi Tanigawa

This building sits on a triangular lot parallel to a river, which is its vanishing point. The structure is the result of blunting the acute angles of the triangular plan that comes from the shape of the lot. In this way, the pyramid roof reaches its optimum volume and the useful surface area is maximized.

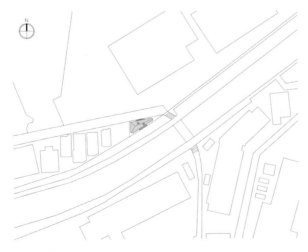

Location plan

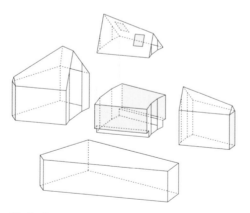

Massing diagrams

Front elevation

Rear elevation

West elevation

Longitudinal section

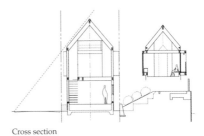

Cross section

The elevation is adjusted to the shape of the lot and follows the flow of the river, making it look like the tip of an arrow.

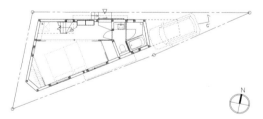

Ground floor plan

N

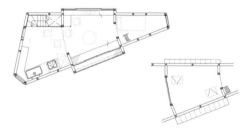

Second floor plan

602 sq. ft. / 56 m²

Peter Kostelov
Moscow, Russia
© Razutdinov Zeynur

The remodeling of this Moscow apartment is intended to breathe new life into a space, adapting it to suit the lifestyle of its new owners. The absence of main walls in the central area allowed it to be shaped by an open wooden structure that stretches, like a geometrically patterned new skin, over the original frame.

This wooden structure creates a sort of inner atrium, arcaded by its top openings, that acts as a hallway and a place to get together.

Small House in Shinjuku

608 sq. ft. / 56.5 m²

Junpei Nousaku Architects
Tokyo, Japan
© Junpei Nousaku Architects

In dense cities like Tokyo, buildings seem to turn their backs on the streets. In an attempt to open up this home to the city, Junpei Nousaku designed a permeable and versatile building: an open atrium where space flows from floor to ceiling and a sense of spaciousness transcends the scale of the actual building.

The kitchen, bedroom and the other service areas are grouped together in the southern part of the home and join in the dining room-atrium with balconies.

Cross and longitudinal sections

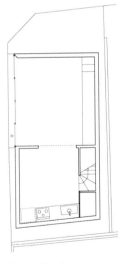

Ground floor plan

Second floor plan

Third floor plan

A web of steel beams crosses the space without fragmenting it, permitting future extensions should the need arise.

635-sq.-ft. Refurbishment

635 sq. ft. / 59 m²

Nir Rothem & Bosmat Sfadia Wolf / SFARO Architects
Tel Aviv, Israel
© Boaz Lavi & Ann Wasserman

With a baby on the way, the configuration of this small family apartment was not practical. In order to add a new bedroom, the interior had to be dismantled and rebuilt, this time leaving a single partition that integrates two existing load-bearing columns and also articulates and unifies the resulting space.

The partition wall unites storage and utilities. Its extremes do not reach the outer walls, allowing 360° movement.

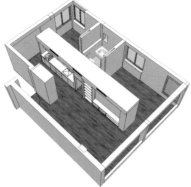

Axonometrics

Floor plan

The bathroom simultaneously functions as a private area — the only one equiped with doors — and also as a secondary passage between rooms.

Fold

645 sq. ft. / 60 m²

Satoshi Kurosaki / APOLLO Architects & Associates
Tokyo, Japan
© Masao Nishikawa

The position of this site, sandwiched between rights of way, led the architects to create an irregularly shaped volume that gives the building a unique touch. The polygonal roof is pleated like origami and gives the interior a compact, yet dynamic and nuanced aspect instead of it being a boring white box.

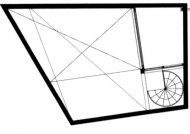

Third floor plan

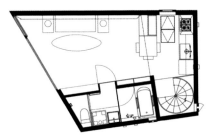

Second floor plan

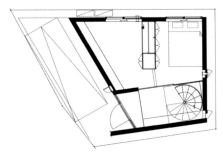

Ground floor plan

The building's angular elevation disperses the
natural illumination entering through the skylights
and adds depth to the space.

Ground and Above Roof House

667 sq. ft. / 62 m²

SPACESPACE
Ibaraki, Japan
© Cortesía de SPACESPACE

The inconspicuous facade of this building only hints at its unique interior. Situated on the border of two different zones, low-rise residential and high-rise residential, the house rises above most of its neighbors. The sleeping quarters and personal space are located in the upper level, and the epicenter of daytime activity is below, with its strange mound visible at street level.

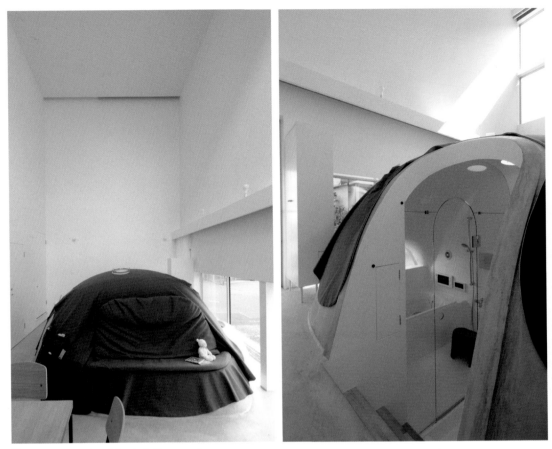

The concrete mound contains the bathroom and helps to complete the needs of the first floor, by acting as a sofa, play area or porch.

The arrangement of the windows and doors is based on the elevation of the surrounding buildings. This allows light to permeate the room and also regulates the temperature.

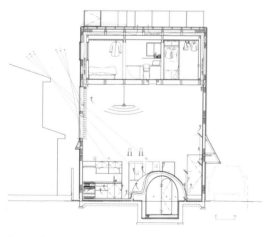

Cross section

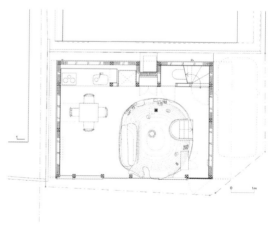

Ground floor plan

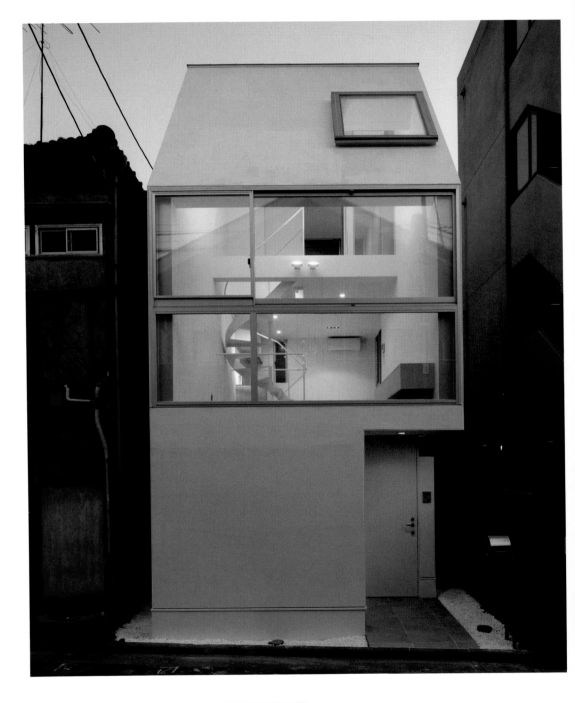

Cielo

678 sq. ft. / 63 m²

Satoshi Kurosaki / APOLLO Architects & Associates
Tokyo, Japan
© Masao Nishikawa

Surrounded by three-storey houses and apartment blocks, the elevation of this home seeks to maximize exposed surface without sacrificing space, while at the same time conforming to the height of its neighbors. Two separate skylights in the facades and side provide light (natural or artificial) and moderate the temperature of the building.

Longitudinal section

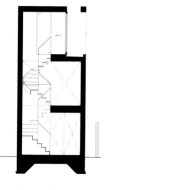

Cross sections

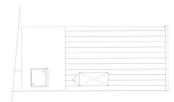

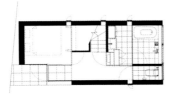

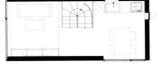

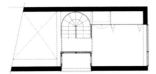

Ground, second, third and roof floor plans

Elevations

The relative opacity of the first floor contrasts with the glowing upper floors. As we ascend, the light seems to amplify the space.

Cubby Home

760 sq. ft. / 70 m²

Edwards Moore
Melbourne, Australia
© Peter Bennetts

The renovation of this apartment makes use of the high ceilings to create a second level for the bedrooms, enabling the lower floor space to be maximized. The furnishings are integrated into the design and help define spaces and provide unity to the ensemble.

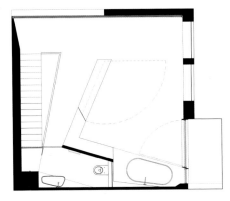

Upper level plan

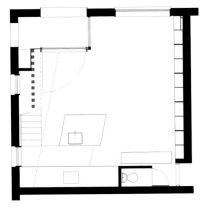

Lower level plan

The glass and glazed handrails allow light from windows and skylights to reach every corner of the hall.

769 sq. ft. / 71.5 m²

Naoto Mitsumoto, Naoko Hamana / mihadesign
Tokyo, Japan
© Sadao Hotta

This Tokyo apartment underwent a drastic renovation to accommodate the needs of a family of six. The original space, with two bedrooms, a kitchen and a dining room, was replaced by two modules of two storeys for the bedrooms and children's areas. This has multiplied the available space by 50 percent.

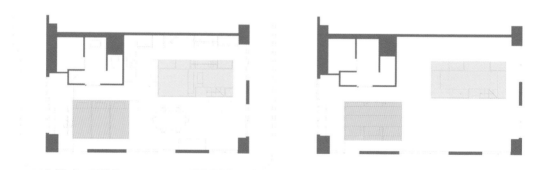

Floor plan

The diagonal arrangement of the modules facilitates smooth movement and helps to define the foyer, kitchen and dining room without isolating them.

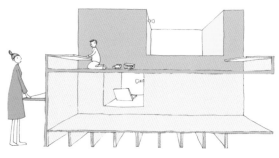

Sketches

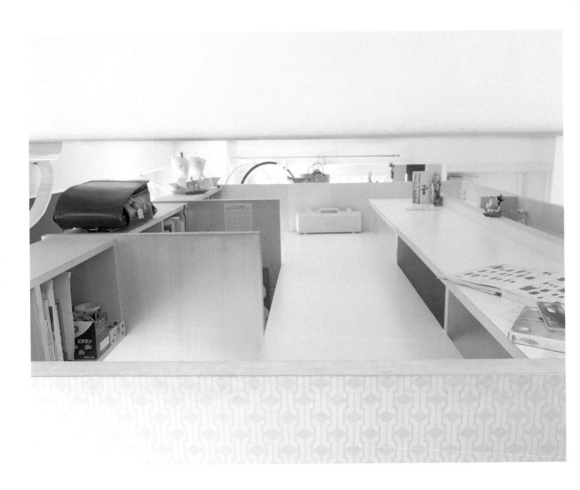

Because they do not reach the ceiling, the modules do not visually close the space. The remaining height (3.6 ft. / 1.1 m) is suitable for children to use.

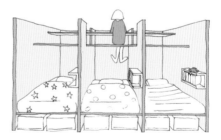

Sketches

Rouge

785 sq. ft. / 73 m²

Satoshi Kurosaki / APOLLO Architects & Associates
Tokyo, Japan
© Koichi Torimura

The client, the manager of a publishing company, wanted to live surrounded by his books and favorite objects. Given his limited budget, the architects decided to incorporate the wooden frame into the design, and to design the floor, ceiling and walls as a single entity that even integrates furniture and fixtures.

Randomly arranged beams of light slip through the windows and skylights, drawing an exquisite contrast with the shady interior.

Lauan, a tropical wood with a streaked, unfinished look, is used here throughout and transforms the room into a cosy cave.

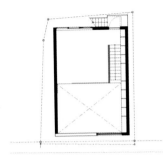

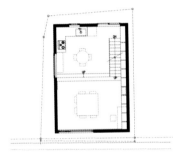

Ground, second and third floor plans

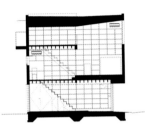

Cross and longitudinal sections

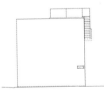

Elevations

Skybox House

807 sq. ft. / 75 m²

Primus architects, atelier + production
Nødebohuse, Denmark
© Tina Krogager

In this small house, the space appears to be segmented into two cubicles joined at one extreme. The smaller one, with a square floor plan, houses the bedrooms, while the larger rectangular cubicle contains the living room, dining room and kitchen. The mixture of low ceilings and huge skylights produces a set of elevations that brings light and spaciousness to the ensemble.

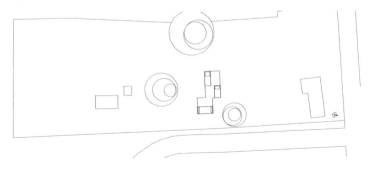

Site plan

The type of plan, together with the positioning of doors and windows, generates cross-sectional views along the entire building.

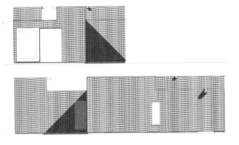

Front elevation

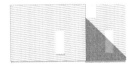

Rear elevation

Floor plan

Container Art Studio

839 sq. ft. / 78 m²

Maziar Behrooz Architecture
Amagansett, U.S.
© Francine Fleischer

This commission consisted of a low-cost art studio annexed to a newly renovated house. It was created by joining two metal shipping containers on concrete foundation walls. Up to two-thirds of the floor was removed in order to move the studio to semi-basement level, giving it a high ceiling.

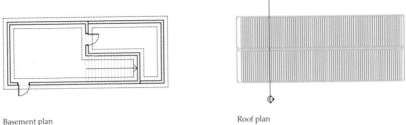

Basement plan

Roof plan

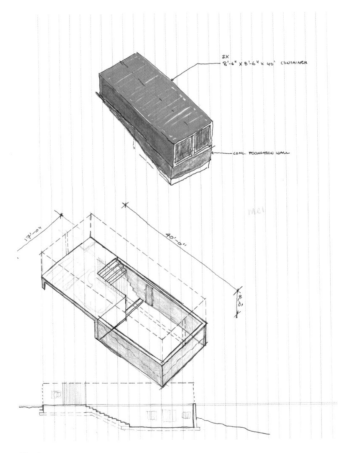

2X
8'-6" X 8'-6" X 40' CONTAINER

CONC. FOUNDATION WALL

17'-0"

40'-0"

Sketch

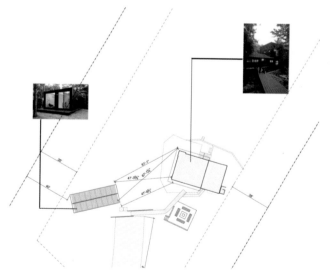

Plan

The two floors, with functions that are clearly differentiated, are connected by a staircase that also functions as an art showcase.

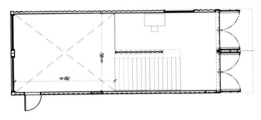

Ground floor plan

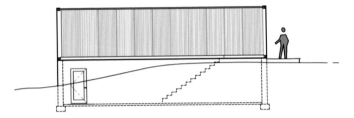

Longitudinal section

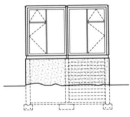
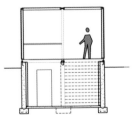

Cross sections

Redeveloper Apartment

850 sq. ft. / 79 m²

Kariouk Associates (with Frédéric Carrier)
Ottawa, Canada
© Christian Lalonde / Photolux Studios

This project avoids the predictable urban housing models that segregate public and private areas. Three elliptical silk-lined volumes hide columns and practical areas and define an open space with areas — dining room, living room and bedroom — that run between a glazed gallery and a wall storage cabinet.

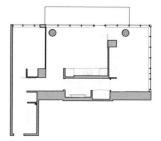

Original floor plan

Floor plan after the renovation

Although the shower is usually a private enclave, in this case it is also a curved glass sculpture with 270° views over the city.

Residence in Kishigawa

850 sq. ft. / 79 m²

Matsunami Mitsutomo
Kishigawa, Japan
© Matsunami Mitsutomo

The owner, a car-loving chef from Wakayama, wanted a well-ventilated home with oblique views of the countryside — and his garage. The solution came in the form of a one-storey building arranged around a central courtyard that serves as access, hallway and atrium, as well as flooding each of the rooms with natural light.

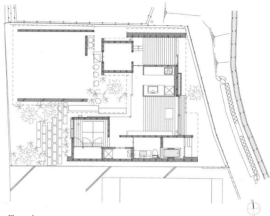

Floor plan

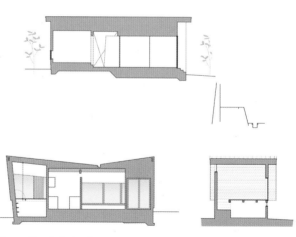

Cross and longitudinal sections

The rather formal planting scheme defines the outside doma steps, obstructing neither movement nor the entry of natural light.

The combination of exterior rice paper panels and
interior curtains is an effective way of isolating
spaces, filtering light and regulating temperature.

Rainy/Sunny

855 sq. ft. / 79.5 m²

Masahiro Harada / Mount Fuji Architects Studio
Tokyo, Japan
© Ryota Atarashi

This house is somewhat experimental. Its architect decided to find the best possible combination of structure and materials to create "a property that lasts forever." To achieve this, he designed a construction system that would reduce the erosion of the materials and adapt to the harshest weather conditions.

The strips on the facade help prevent erosion of the concrete. A larch mold was used to imprint a wood texture on the surface.

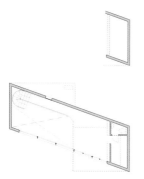

Ground / second floor plan

Longitudinal section

The glass wall insulates the interior without visually closing it off from the exterior. Similar wood has been used for the porch and the parquet flooring, blending the two spaces.

Mur

861 sq. ft. / 80 m²

Satoshi Kurosaki / APOLLO Architects & Associates
Yokohama, Japan
© Masao Nishikawa

The facade of this house has had an inevitable effect on its interior design. Its walls surround a courtyard, with rooms arranged around it. Resembling an open shoebox, this structure is so simple and effective that it makes the building a delicate exercise in balance between privacy and transparency.

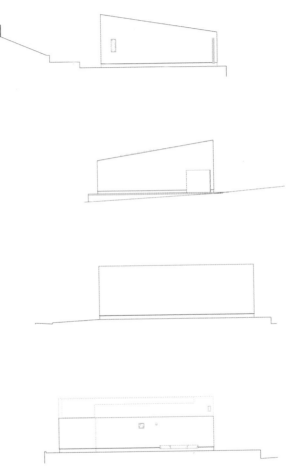

Elevations

The glazed gallery, which opens onto the porch, allows the master bedroom to be insulated and ventilated without ever blocking the entry of natural light.

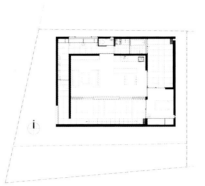

Floor plan

Elevations

Elevations

Storage House

882 sq. ft. / 82 m²

Ryuji Fujimura Architects
Kanagawa, Japan
© Takumi Ota

Although its sterile, steely appearance resembles a bunker, this building is actually a refined exercise in rationalism. The section dominates the plan. Instead of overlapping, the floors are arranged to achieve the optimal spatial configuration without sticking to a vertical hierarchy.

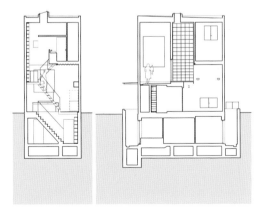

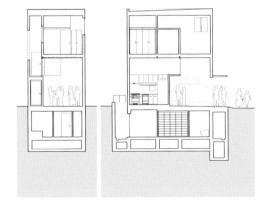

Cross sections

Occupying the central space, the staircase houses a wooden bookcase that extends over three floors and culminates in a loft.

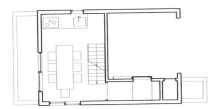

Ground floor plan

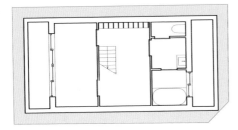

Basement plan

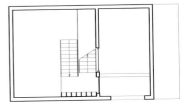

Fourth floor plan

Third floor plan

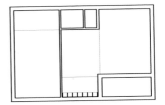

Second floor plan

Gate

947 sq. ft. / 88 m²

Naoto Mitsumoto, Naoko Hamana / mihadesign
Tokyo, Japan
© Sadao Hotta

The narrowness and height regulations of the lot on which this house was built were tackled by dividing it into four "horizontal planes" separated by three supporting walls. From south to north, each unit signals a new level of intimacy: the public spaces are near the entrance and the bedroom and the bathroom are toward the back.

Longitudinal section

This zigzag roof allows the maximum exterior area of sunshine. Skylights collect light that scatters through the open interior.

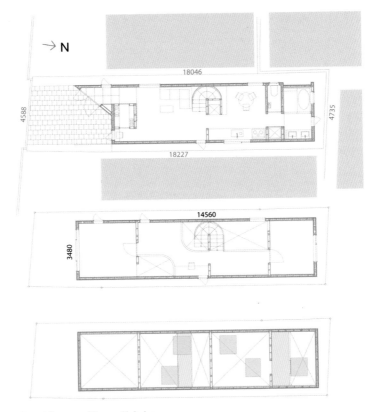

Ground floor, second floor and loft plan

Ring

957 sq. ft. / 89 m²

Satoshi Kurosaki / APOLLO Architects & Associates
Tokyo, Japan
© Masao Nishikawa

A daring ring-shaped cantilever is the hallmark of this home. This "hood" creates a transition zone between the exterior and interior. A rigid steel frame holds its wooden structure in place and makes the continuous set of windows on the south facade possible.

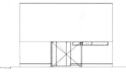

Elevations

The second floor is a space for the family to get
together. The sloping roof is projected toward the
cantilever, unifying the room.

Second floor plan

Ground floor plan

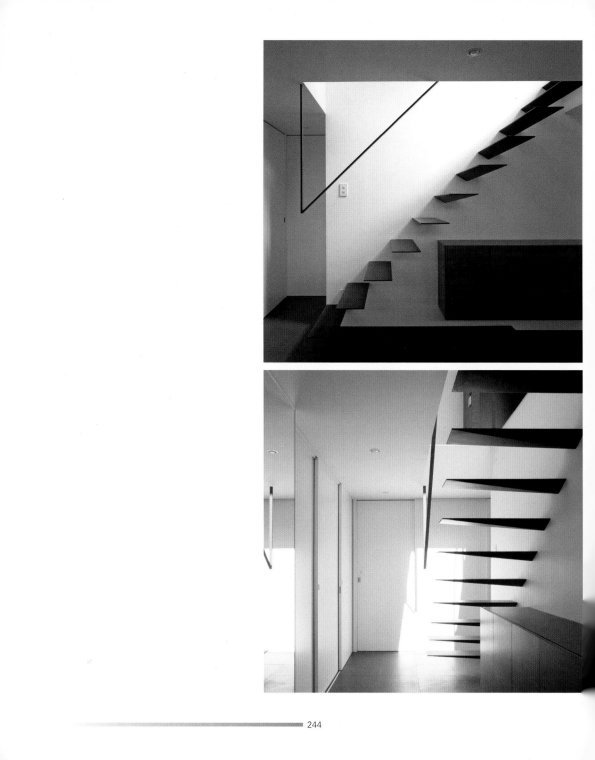

From above, the cantilever frames the sky and blocks the view of the chaotic urban landscape. On the balcony, the grid flooring acts as a lattice.

Loft Conversion in Terronská

958 sq. ft. / 89 m²

Dalibor Hlaváček / idhea
Prague, Czech Republic
© Dalibor Hlaváček

Making this attic space habitable required maximizing available space and refraining from using a plethora of color. The slope of this space led to the design having an isosceles triangle plan with the most "heavy" elements — kitchen, bedroom and bathroom — crowded into the base so that the entire ceiling was visible in other areas.

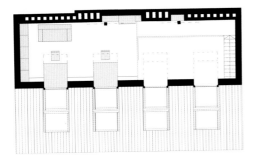

Upper level plan

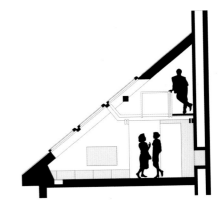

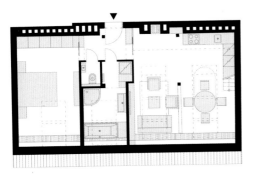

Lower level plan

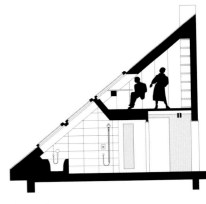

Cross sections

The stairway is also a bridge that leads to the veranda and the kitchen. The bookshelves and boiler are to be found in the space between the chimneys.

On the roof, four groups of three energy-efficient glass windows minimize the need for artificial light and help to create a fresh atmosphere.